THE PHYSICIAN'S GUIDE TO ACHIEVING FINANCIAL FREEDOM USING STOCKS AND OPTIONS

How I Became Financially Free Using a Simple 3-Step Stock Investing Process

CHRISTOPHER H. LOO, MD-Phd

Copyright © 2019 Christopher H. Loo

All Rights Reserved

Paperback ISBN: 978-1-0912-9472-1

Hardback ISBN: 979-8-4280-6146-8

Disclaimer: I do not offer financial advice, services, or products. This is my personal investment plan, method. I am merely here to educate, give the reader a better understanding of the investing-trading process as a whole. I am giving you a glimpse into how I achieved financial independence and freedom. I have compiled the best ideas I received from *How to Make Money in Stocks, Reminiscences of a Stock Operator, One Up on Wall Street,* and *Battle for Investment Survival*, among others.

I use investing and trading interchangeably, although investing is more of a long-term strategy, and trading is more of a short-term strategy.

I am not a tax attorney or advisor, so consult a tax attorney and/or advisor for any legal and/or tax advice.

This book is dedicated to God, my parents, Sue Hwa and Lian Sim Loo, my wife Annie Phu, my brother Nathaniel H. Loo, MD, my nieces and nephew, Tiffany, Sophia, Aubrey, Tina, Olivia, Sabrina, Kai, and to all of my clients (past, current, and future) who have entrusted or will entrust me with their lives, in the hopes of better, brighter futures.

Books by Christopher H. Loo

How I Quit My Lucrative Medical Career and Achieved Financial Freedom Using Real Estate (You Can, Too!)

The Physician's Guide to Financial Freedom Using Stocks and Options

The Physician's Guide to Financial Freedom: Getting Started as a Consultant

The Physician's Guide to Financial Freedom: Becoming a Freelance Writer

THE PHYSICANS GUIDE TO ACHIEVING FINANCIAL FREEDOM USING STOCKS AND OPTIONS

CONTENTS

INTRODUCTION _____ 3
CHAPTER 1: MY STORY _____ 14
CHAPTER 2: HOW I GOT STARTED IN STOCKS _____ 19
CHAPTER 3: THE PSYCHOLOGY OF INVESTING AND
  TRADING IN THE MARKETS _____ 24
  Different types of biases _____ 25
  Harnessing your psychology for optimal performance
  _____ 31
  My daily routine _____ 33
CHAPTER 4: STOCKS _____ 36
  How to select stocks _____ 37
  My 3-step process for investing in stocks that made me
    financially free _____ 42
  Volatility _____ 44
CHAPTER 5: GETTING STARTED _____ 48
  Sources of information _____ 48

Opening up a brokerage account	49
General mindset: what you're looking for	50
How to Read a Chart	51
CHAPTER 6: USING OPTIONS IN YOUR PORTFOLIO	54
CHAPTER 7: MONEY MANAGEMENT	63
Risk and Management	64
Important ideas	66
Setting rules for money management	66
Tax saving strategies with a Roth IRA and solo 401(k)	67
CONCLUSION	69
ABOUT THE AUTHOR	73

INTRODUCTION

SO, YOU HATE your job. You can't stand your boss. You can't stand your co-workers. You're sick and tired of the daily monotony, trading your time for a paycheck.

You sit there and watch the clock, waiting for it turn to 5:00. You're sick and tired of waking up at 5 a.m., getting stuck in rush-hour traffic, just to get into the office by 9 a.m.

You're tired of the fakeness.

You're tired of the lack of authenticity in the corporate world. The hypocrisy.

You feel like a cog in the wheel, a slave.

You come home tired, exhausted, feeling like you've wasted the day.

You long to travel, to contribute to charity, to run a marathon, pursue your passions, learn, and grow, to face your fears, to create, and to go after your dream.

You feel like, if you worked as hard on your own job, you could be five times more successful than your boss.

You're not alone. I felt the same way in 2007. I thought I had it all. An MD from a top-notch medical school. A coveted orthopedic surgery residency. *But* it was all a mask—to cover up my insecurities, my fears, what other people thought of me. I was trying to fit into society's molds and standards, trying to please others and manipulate their way of thinking about me—and, oftentimes, they didn't even really care. That was my perception.

And with each success or accolade I attained back then, my ego became bigger and bigger, and I added layer upon layer of masks around that ego I was building, which further separated me from others. (This was the opposite effect I was trying to achieve, which was to be accepted.)

Here's the reality: the world is changing—*EXPONENTIALLY*. Jobs are not meant to serve you; you are meant to serve the corporation, your boss. Government jobs are no longer safe or secure, either.

Here's another part of reality: the educational system is designed to educate the working force, a group of people who will say yes, work hard, follow the rules, work together, be loyal, and produce results for their boss/company. And there is nothing wrong with that—if that's what you love to do. However, if you step outside of the box, it is a different story.

The system does not reward questioning the status quo, questioning hierarchy, questioning authority, being independent, innovating, being creative, disruption, new technology, or outside-the-box thinking. Consider Steve Jobs, Bill Gates, Mark Zuckerberg, Michael Dell… The list goes on and on.

Millions and millions of people are now waking up to this new reality.

Some sure ways you will get fired from your job:

- ✓ If you don't do your job. Period.
- ✓ If you don't do your job and your boss hates you, or your superiors or co-workers can't stand you.
- ✓ If you're lazy, unreliable, unprofessional, rude, mean, can't work well with others, don't listen to higher authority.
- ✓ If you come in late, leave early.

If you're any of these, but you do your job, you may be okay for a while. But, in my opinion, your days are numbered. Every circumstance is different, though.

Some other ways that a corporate career is not suited for you:

- ✓ If you do your job (even if you excel at it) but cause trouble, gossip, sabotage, backstab others.
- ✓ People don't like you.
- ✓ You make people, especially your boss, feel insecure.
- ✓ If you speak up.
- ✓ If you think or act differently.

In the examples above, you may not get fired right away (depending upon the company, boss, situation, and circumstances), but you may hit a plateau, a ceiling.

The Peter Principle states that people in the corporate world rise up to their highest level of incompetence, which explains why the majority of senior management in huge corporations and bureaucracies are usually deemed "incompetent" by everyone except for their peers and bosses, who placed them in those roles. The boss's role is to make sure they keep employees in line, and execute C-level tasks and priorities.

Jobs are meant to keep you stuck and serving the corporation. The educational system is designed to make you a corporate cog, an employee who follows and obeys the rules. Again, these are all old, outdated remnants of Baby Boomer, Gen X, and Industrial Age ideas.

Over two thirds of people are unsatisfied in their current roles or occupations!

Over ninety percent of people are living unfulfilled, stuck, bored, meaningless lives! Especially in the United States, the most powerful, wealthy and abundant country with the most opportunity in the world.

How can this be!?!?

My dream growing up was to become a doctor so I could have a stable, secure, high-status job that I thought was going to be challenging and rewarding.

Instead, I learned that it was a career fraught with endless bureaucratic rules and regulations, created by politicians, administrators, bureaucrats, personnel, fake and disingenuous people, backstabbers, and passive-aggressiveness. Nobody was interested in doing the right thing. Everybody was concerned with keeping their jobs, keeping their heads down, and being "yes" men.

Patients didn't give a damn if you did a good job or not. They continued to destroy their lives, their health, and their bodies, and then they tried to sue doctors for not taking responsibility for their own actions. They often lacked appreciation for what doctors did and took advantage of the system. Patients lied, cheated, and stole from the system. At the same time, hospital executives, administrators, insurance, pharma, politicians, and lawyers also continued to take advantage of the system.

BUT times are changing, exponentially and fast. Did you know that...

An individual in Africa will have access to a cell phone before he/she has access to running water, modern housing, and ample food?

People are no longer buying houses; instead, they are opting to rent. A house is no longer an "asset."

People are no longer taking on excessive student-loan debt. The value of a traditional education is being called into question.

Khan Academy is revolutionizing learning and education through its online platforms. It is democratizing a world-class education (Harvard, MIT, Stanford, Princeton, and other Ivy League schools) and making it available to the masses for free.

In the future, core competencies will be emphasized more than grades, and every graduate will soon have a portfolio of work in their area of expertise. Many companies and corporations have an "audition" or a portfolio of work you must show, in order to get hired.

Google, Tesla, Apple, and Facebook no longer rely solely on the institution you came from in their hiring decisions or on the grades you received.

Our social, economic, political, and financial systems are in upheaval, disruption. Look at the recent Trump government shutdown to help fund the wall along the US-Mexico border, during which multitudes of government employees chose not to show up for work, because there was no approved budget to pay them, so they opted instead to drive for Uber and Lyft.

Clerical, automated tasks (airports, truck drivers, servers, minimum-wage jobs) will be reassigned to robots and machines in the next ten to fifteen years, maybe even sooner.

The future will belong to creatives, visionaries, and innovators who possess key valuable skillsets.

Knowledge-based workers, like lawyers and doctors or those in the sectors of accounting and finance, will see their industries rapidly change over the next decade.

People aren't willing to put in the time to climb the corporate ladder. More and more freelancers and entrepreneurs work from home or from anywhere in the world.

People are getting married at a later age, are getting married multiple times over their lives, are no longer getting married, or are having multiple partners.

People are switching to multiple careers and jobs during their lifetimes.

Millionaire and billionaire status is no longer age-reserved, or limited to level of education, nationality, race, or any sort of barrier you can name. You no longer need excess capital or a fancy-expensive pedigree to make it in this world.

Happiness and fulfillment are no longer a rosy picture painted by society or the media. They now depend on individual standards.

People are electing not to have kids or are having only one child.

So, where in the past it was the pain of failure/rejection that kept people from taking action, now, with the myriad options and opportunities and lower barriers to entry, it is the pain of regret for not starting and the fear of missing out that should be the primary driver.

The pain of regret is worse than the pain of rejection, failure, humiliation, embarrassment, or loss, because the number of opportunities in today's society is limitless.

###

CHAPTER 1

MY STORY

WHEN I WAS GROWING up, the key to a stable, secure, successful life was to become a highly paid specialist. One of the ways was to do that was through becoming a highly educated, specialized physician. After all, everybody needs health. Health is a commodity. If you're a physician, you are set, right?

In most cases, yes. But if you do it for the wrong reasons, then the hassles and struggles may not be worth your while, and you'd probably be better off and happier doing other things. Instead of wasting your time, struggling in a career you do not love, you might be better off pursuing other ambitions, chasing your dreams. I tell my private coaching clients this all the time: it's better to be successful at something that makes you happy instead of being successful at something that makes you miserable.

So, a lot of physicians get "trapped." They buy the million-dollar house, five fancy cars, private schools for their children, expensive clothing and shoes, and cosmetic surgeries. They are working hard, generating a lot of income, yet paying millions of dollars in taxes over their lifetimes, with little to no savings. If anything were to occur that prevented them from doing their job, their financial futures would be in dire straits.

This not only happens to physicians but also to highly paid specialists, consultants, investment bankers, lawyers—you name it. Any career where you are tied to your job. You may love or enjoy every second of the job, but it is not true freedom. True freedom is being able to walk away at any point and not have any obligations whatsoever. Even if you own your own business, you may not be truly free, if you're tied to that business.

You should be making more money to earn you more time. Most people spend their entire lives earning a living, only to realize at the end of their lives they wish they had more time.

The only way to have true freedom is to:

- ➢ Separate your time from your income generators.
- ➢ Invest in assets that provide passive income (real estate, stocks, writing).
- ➢ Become a business owner and entrepreneur—leveraging people, assets, time, money, and resources.

And that's what this book is about. It's about keying in on the idea of using paper assets (stocks and options) to generate multiple streams of passive income so you never have to work another day in your life, or, if you do, you do it because you want to do it. Purpose and passion over being solely income-driven.

So, what are some potential ways of generating passive income?

- ✓ Starting or owning a business—consulting, public speaking, blog, vlog, social media, coaching
- ✓ Owning a franchise
- ✓ Real estate
- ✓ Stocks
- ✓ Writing books

This book will focus on investing in paper assets as an alternate source of passive income.

Who is this book for? (OR some reasons that you'd want to use stock-options)

You may want to:

- ✓ Diversify your passive income streams (have at least ten).
- ✓ Want the convenience of buying-selling paper assets (easy liquidity) as opposed to

buying-selling an actual business, real estate, or franchise.
- ✓ Convenience.
- ✓ Love for the financial markets.
- ✓ As a tax saving strategy.
- ✓ Hedge against inflation.
- ✓ Strategy for income, wealth generation, financial freedom, and independence.

###

CHAPTER 2

HOW I GOT STARTED IN STOCKS

IT WAS 2001. It was post 9-11. WorldCom and Enron had declared bankruptcy. Giants were falling. I got a "tip" to invest in Enron...

That was one of my worst decisions. At that time, it had fallen from its all-time highs in the eighties and nineties to less than a dollar per share. I naively sent my broker $1,000 to invest in shares of the now-defunct company. A few months later, I logged into my account and my balance was 0!

I felt horrified. What had happened?! I felt cheated, ripped off, scammed. But that was my victim-self talking. I was 100% responsible for what had happened. I had made the decision.

I also had a significant sum invested in mutual funds, which saw a fifty percent decrease after the tech market bust. After I educated myself, I discovered that these "funds" were the most expensive ones—front and back load, and sold by my investment "advisor," who was really just a sales agent who made a commission by directing funding to the brokerage's funds so they would be able to receive hefty commissions.

I was dumbstruck at how stupid I'd been, that I had no experience and people were profiting from it. Luckily, as my funds recovered, I sold them, fired my broker, invested in my own education, and since then haven't looked back.

$1,000 may or may not be a lot of money to you, but, as a student, while losing $1,000 wasn't the end of the world, it was no laughing matter, either. At least I had $1,000 to invest...

But it was the best thing to "happen" to me, because it forced me to face reality and start to educate myself, instead of listening to a sales broker, who called himself an "advisor."

I was pissed at how little financial education I had, allowing people to profit off of my ignorance. And it wasn't just me; it was the entire country.

I channeled that anger and rage into productive channels. I started to read more about financials and learned how to invest in stocks; I actively studied the economy and the market. This led me to read the work of Robert Kiyosaki, Tony Robbins, and other mega-influencers we know today. And these years of study turned me from someone who knew nothing about investing and investments into someone who coaches others about how to educate themselves about investing.

Although, I do not recommend certain investments, I teach investment psychology, strategy, and mechanics. I turned my ignorance into an asset by becoming someone who was well-educated, in control, and responsible for his own actions. I vowed never to let that happen again. Which is why I am writing this book.

I became financially free at the age of twenty-nine, using the principles I'm going to describe in this book during the peak of the real estate crisis; I weathered the 2008 downturn and have profited from the bull run since 2009. The market has definitely changed. It is more volatile, unpredictable, and uncertain. What worked ten years ago doesn't always work in today's market. So, you have to be careful, and you have to educate yourself.

What I am going to share with you is my blueprint, system, and strategy for succeeding in the market. I will lay out the tools, resources, and skillsets involved in how I invest in stocks. I'll describe how I was able to lay out a 3-step process in stock investing and become financially free at the age of twenty-nine, so I could free up my time to pursue my true calling and true passions.

What I've learned are simple strategies that, if executed with the right mental state, including belief, certainty, clarity, discipline, and patience, will ensure you, too, can come out ahead. You don't have to time the market. You don't need any fancy techniques, tricks, or magic crystal balls. But it does take knowledge, information, education, discipline, and execution.

Much like top athletes or top performers in any profession, investing is both a mindset and a skill set.

Did you ever notice how top athletes, when they lose their mental focus and composure, also see their performance decline? It is pretty much guaranteed they will lose at that level of competition.

The top investors and traders have coaches. You want to operate, perceive, think, and feel from a place of certainty, a peak state, despite the circumstances.

###

CHAPTER 3

THE PSYCHOLOGY OF INVESTING AND TRADING IN THE MARKETS

THE TWO PRIMARY drivers in the market are:

1. Fear: fear of loss, fear of missing out

2. Greed: wanting more.

These two primary emotional drivers cause us to buy at the wrong times (peaks, bubbles, media hype) and sell at the worst times, too.

They also cause us to get into investments that have high downside risk and little upside potential, but, because of greed, we make poor decisions.

Warren Buffett's famous line is this: "Be greedy when others are fearful, and be fearful when others are greedy." This statement translates to mean know your tendencies, your goals, and the outcomes you want in life. Don't compare yourself to anyone else. Stay in your lane. Make informed decisions. Do your investment homework. Stick to a plan, a process. Despite what is going on around you, you have to stick to a plan or strategy, to realize optimal performance.

So, when everybody is selling, you should be buying. And when everybody is buying, you should be selling.

Different types of biases

There are twenty-five types of cognitive biases that affect behavioral decisions in finance. A great YouTube video is titled *The Psychology of Human Misjudgment—25 Cognitive Biases* by Charlie Munger, Harvard University.

These biases cause us to make decisions, either good or bad. It is our job to understand these biases and how they influence our daily investment decisions.

The key here is that there are factors and influences operating beyond our conscious awareness that influence our emotions, which, in turn, influence our thoughts, perceptions, behaviors, and actions. It is our ability to become aware of these underlying processes that may or may not be hindering or helping our specific results and outcomes.

Bias 1: **Reward and punishment super-response tendency.** Using incentives and disincentives to affect behavioral outcomes

Bias 2: **Liking-loving tendency.** A bias toward those we like and/or love

Bias 3: **Disliking-hating tendency.** Bias against those whom we dislike and/or hate.

Bias 4: Doubt-avoidance tendency. When in doubt, we try to remove doubt by making an ill-informed, quick decision.

Bias 5: Inconsistency-avoidance tendency. See below.

Bias 6: Curiosity tendency. Tendency to look into the unknown and unfamiliar; creating innovation and driving progress throughout human history.

Bias 7: Kantian fairness tendency. Tolerating a little unfairness in life is worth it, if it results in fairness for all.

Bias 8: Envy-jealousy tendency. See below.

Bias 9: Reciprocation tendency. Tendency to return the favor.

Bias 10: Influence-from-mere-association tendency. Tendency to be swayed one way or the other via mere association

Bias 11: Simple, pain-avoiding psychological denial. Tendency to distort the facts so they become bearable.

Bias 12: Excessive self-regard tendency. See below

Bias 13: Over-optimism. Tendency to think that over-optimism is the normal human condition.

Bias 14: Deprival super-reaction. See below.

Bias 15: Social proof tendency. See below.

Bias 16: Contrast-misreaction tendency. Tendency to view comparisons based on their contrast versus looking objectively at themselves (for example, doubling the listing price, but then offering a fifty-percent reduction, which is actually the standard price).

Bias 17: Stress-influence tendency. A little stress is good for performance, but too much leads to poor performance and dysfunction.

Bias 18: Use-it-or-lose-it tendency. Skills attenuate with disuse.

Bias 19: Availability mis-weighing tendency. The mind uses what is easily available and discounts what it can't easily recognize or remember.

Bias 20: Drug mis-influence tendency. Tendency for distraction/numbing yourself, instead of doing the right thing.

Bias 21: Senescence-mis-influence tendency. Continuous learning and thinking helps to curb the natural loss of skills and abilities from aging and disuse.

Bias 22: Authority-mis-influence tendency. "Because he or she said so"; following orders.

Bias 23: Twaddle tendency. Tendency to spend too much time on nonsense and procrastination (workaholism, social media, pornography, drugs, gambling, drinking, smoking, eating, TV, shopping—you name it).

Bias 24: Reason-respective tendency. People don't want to think about the reasoning or understanding behind an idea; they just want the answers.

Bias 25: Lollapalooza tendency. Tendency to get some of the other twenty-four cognitive biases together in order to achieve a particular outcome (for example, authority, social proof, scarcity-stress).

The key point here is that, although their names sound fancy, we want to pay attention to how they affect investing-trading behavior. This is a fascinating section, because these twenty-five cognitive biases govern how we behave at an unconscious level. There are numerous examples throughout business, politics, relationships, and finance.

Let me highlight next the five most common to affect investing-trading behavior.

1. *Deprival super-reaction tendency.* This is the tendency for people to strongly prefer avoiding losses (fear) over acquiring gains (towards actions). This translates into people holding on too long to a losing stock and missing out on future potential gains. Or they get out too early and fail to let the stock ride.

2. *Excessive self-regard tendency.* This causes people to be too overconfident.

3. *Inconsistency avoidance.* This leads to not modifying or tailoring your strategy in order to keep up with the market. It comes from a reluctance to change bad habits.

4. *Envy-jealousy tendency.* This translates into trying to get rich quick and keep up with the Joneses.

5. *Social proof tendency.* This is the following-the-herd crowd. And crowd behavior leads to manias, bubbles (tech, real estate, Bitcoin) and panics.

Harnessing your psychology for optimal performance

No doubt, your psychology and mental state influence your outcomes, particularly investing-trading in the stock market.

Being a top investor or trader is not unlike being a top athlete, musician, surgeon, lawyer, writer, or entrepreneur. It is important to be in a peak mental state, in order to make the best-informed decisions. I have routines and rituals that make me more effective and that put me in the zone on a consistent basis.

The routines and rituals of high powered and highly effective individuals tend to get you on track without thinking about it. They help relieve you of mental clutter and draining energy, bolster your will power, and set you up for living a successful day.

The morning is the best time to get things done. Your body is its best at this time of day. But for some, it's the wee hours of the night. Whatever it is, develop a routine where you are locked into a high-performing, high-impact pattern of behavior. Ideally, you are able to run on autopilot. Once you program and condition your mind for high-performance habits, it takes less energy.

Daniel Kahneman, author of *Thinking Fast, Thinking Slow*, says there are two neural pathways—the fast and the slow. The fast is the intuitive, automatic path and takes less energy. We need to train, program, and condition our minds to incorporate these high-impact patterns of thinking, perception, feeling, believing, and action into our daily habits, so they become automatic and ingrained in us.

My daily routine

1. Drink 500 cc of water (the body generally has been without water for eight-plus hours overnight)

2. Wake up at 5-6:00 a.m.

3. Do a two- to three-mile run

4. Have a one- to two-minute icy-cold shower

5. Do thirty minutes of meditation, focusing on my intentions, and doing visualizations

6. Breakfast

7. Ninety minutes, broken down into ten-minute chunks

8. Identify the one or two most important things to accomplish that day.

9. Once those are completed, shut off all technology.

10. Then, I run eight to ten miles, go to a coffee shop, maybe hang out with friends.

Here are the things I invest in:

- ✓ People
- ✓ Friendships
- ✓ Relationships
- ✓ Professional contacts
- ✓ Access
- ✓ Experiences
- ✓ Education
- ✓ Knowledge
- ✓ Ideas
- ✓ Information
- ✓ Resources
- ✓ Tools
- ✓ Travel
- ✓ Peak experiences
- ✓ Growth

I do not overconsume on cars, clothing, or fancy houses. I do splurge occasionally on things like nice hotels, restaurants, spas, or travelling first class. I value first-rate experiences, education, access, information, and freedom over physical things.

###

CHAPTER 4

STOCKS

THIS BOOK IS FOCUSED on generating multiple streams of passive income using stocks.

I will show you the different sectors and how to evaluate a stock based on fundamentals and technicals. I will show you how to analyze a stock based on chart patterns; how to define certain entry and exit points; how to analyze a stock based on dividends; how much capital to allocate; how to save on taxes using a personal 401k or Roth IRA; and how to select which brokerage firm to work with.

I'll also look at the infinite strategies for evaluating, selecting, and mitigating risk using options inside your portfolio.

How to select stocks

Stocks are an important asset class in which I like to invest and trade.

I love the liquidity of this asset. I get a thrill out of analyzing and researching a stock, including its price points, the highs and lows, its range, and its value or P/E ratio.

I love buying the products of popular stocks, like AAPL, SBUX, and Nike.

I love going from being a consumer of products to an investor in publicly traded companies.

I love the idea of huge tax savings for long-term investors. Warren Buffett is one of the wealthiest men alive by being a long-term investor and employing huge tax saving strategies.

I love the idea of investing in dividend-reinvestment programs and, after reinvesting, seeing the power of compounding returns.

I love the ability to buy and sell stocks and options. Best of all, it means not dealing with contracts, mortgages, inspections, appraisals, and other real estate hassles. There are no tenants or improvements. Each of us has total control over our research, price, and entry points.

The stock market has something for everyone. There are a wide variety of choices, from blue-chip stocks to tech stocks, health care stocks, medical device, pharma, aviation, and so on.

There are also an infinite number of strategies available to traders (short-term) and investors (long-term) offering variety and diversity.

That being said, there are multiple challenges, such as applying the right strategy at the right time. A challenge can arise if you buy too high or sell too low, or if you get caught in the crowd/herd mentality. Sometimes, there are market crashes.

Some people see the stock market as a "casino." These concerns are indeed valid, given the volatility and extensive change in the market over the past eighteen years. Now, we have the impact of computer algorithms, large institutions, and hedge funds that control the volume and direction of trading.

I believe that every individual should have equities as a portion of their portfolio for multiple reasons: long term investment, easy liquidity, compounding returns, capital preservation, keeping pace with inflation, growth, and as part of their strategy for becoming financially independent and wealthy.

So, how do you get started, given this abundance of choices and cautionary tales?

Disclaimer first: I am sharing only my experiences, failures, and successes. I do not have a finance background, degree, or any certifications. I only have real-world experience. That said, I am going to show you a simple three-step process for becoming financially free using the stock market.

The first three things to do when deciding to invest or trade in stocks is:

1. Determine your goals.

- Are they long- or short-term?
- What is your time horizon? (one day, one week, one month, one year, or ten years?) Are you looking for a quick flip? Or are you looking to put a certain amount away each and every month?
- How involved do you want to be? (mutual funds, ETFs, stocks, and options—each requires a different degree of engagement and supervision)
- How much capital do you have?
- How much do you want to invest in a particular stock?

2. Know your risk profile.

This goes without saying. If you have a low risk profile, avoid extremely volatile, actively traded stocks. Invest for the long term, where you allocate a certain amount each month.

Conversely, if you're more of a conservative investor, invest in blue-chip stocks—MSFT, WMT, MCD, and so on. Invest a certain amount every month in a stable, low-cost index fund.

3. Know yourself.

Because there is so much diversity and so many options out there in the stock market, knowing yourself, your goals, and your risk profile are paramount, in order to avoid losing money. There are so many "experts" telling you to invest in this and that. You want to get clear where you stand after factoring in wisdom and information.

Investing is a combination of mindset and skillset. It is a disciplined way of allocating your money and letting it grow. Always invest for the long term.

- ✶ Rule #1: Never invest in something that you don't understand (Warren Buffett).
- ✶ Rule #2: Do not lose money (Warren Buffett, Ray Dalio).

People think you get into investing to "make money," but the reality is you must protect your downside first (aka never losing money).

My 3-step process for investing in stocks that made me financially free

Step 1: Set aside a certain portion or percentage of your monthly income towards "paying yourself first."

Step 2: Choose an index fund with the lowest fees and expenses.

Step 3: Reinvest the dividends.

Step 4: Wash, rinse, and repeat.

The amount you set aside depends upon the following:

- Your income level
- Your expense levels

I recommend "paying yourself first," setting aside ten percent or even more.

With the amount of turmoil and change in today's society and given the number of "jobs" being disrupted, there is no better or more important time to get your finances in order.

In general, I try to save and/or invest eighty percent of my income (on the high side). That will vary, based upon each individual's needs and wants, of course.

At a minimum, it is recommended you put ten percent of your income toward savings and/or investments. Of that ten percent:

> ➤ One-third should be in a safety security basket.
> ➤ One third should be in a growth basket.
> ➤ One third goes toward your dream basket.

Also, in general, it is recommended that you have, in savings, an amount equal to three to six months' worth of expenses. Personally, I recommend having two years' worth.

I also recommend you hold physical assets, including gold and silver, regardless of the misreported inflation figures of two percent.

Some people prefer to have a big house. That's perfectly fine, although it does come with high property taxes, repairs, and other costs. I prefer to live comfortably in a nice neighborhood and use my extra funds to help others, donate to charity, travel, and dine out with my wife and family. I value time, freedom, low hassle, and experiences over the excessive hassles and worries that the extra income entails.

Volatility

A note about stock market "volatility." Studies show that a bear market (which means any dip greater than twenty percent) happens once every three to five years and can last anywhere from a month to a year to several years. But studies also show that, in the past one hundred years, the stock market has *always* increased. It will only decrease if economic activity ceases.

Market corrections of greater than ten percent happen approximately once a year and usually last several months.

Given the fact that market corrections, bear markets, will occur and can be short- or long-lived, and given that the Dow will invariably recover (it has to, because economic activity would cease to exist, should it not), the key idea here is to set aside a certain amount of money (not all of it) and invest at regularly scheduled intervals.

During down times, you buy more shares. During good times, you buy fewer. But, overall, the shares will continue to grow and produce dividends, which will be reinvested and compounded. This is how Warren Buffett and Charlie Munger have become some of the wealthiest men on the planet: by buying value, reinvesting the dividends, and saving on taxes (among other things).

That being said, the market is much more volatile now compared to prior decades, due to technology, globalization, information, institutional investing, hedge funds' high-frequency trading, robo-/AI-driven trading, and front running. But again, we are talking about long-term investing and not short-term trading.

I had to learn this lesson the hard way. First, with the tech boom of 1999-2000, and then in the real estate boom/bust of 2007-2009. In the bull market of 2009 to the present, the Dow has increased from 7,500 all the way to over 26,000 (as of this writing). And this is after dropping from 10,000 to 7,500 (the dot-com bubble) and from 14,000 to 8,400 (real estate bubble).

So, if you had just left your money in or bought during the bear markets (i.e., accumulated more shares, and invested in dividend as well as growth funds, and then reinvested those profits), you would have turned out just fine.

Here's the key: timing the market does not work. Have you ever bought a share and then had it go down, sold it at a loss, and then watched the stock price rise to levels you never even imagined? Or how about bought a share in a company, sold it at a profit, and then watched it climb higher? Frustrating, isn't it?

That's why one of the strategies we need is to regularly invest a certain portion of our income: for our nest egg, for long-term growth. In all of these cycles, amidst all of this turmoil, and through all of these environments of fear, the market came out on top at the end of the eighteen years.

And keep in mind your personal time horizon, as that is the fourth thing to consider when deciding to invest or trade in stocks. A person in their twenties may be able to afford a greater loss and make it up over time as opposed to a person who is starting out as a trader or investor in their fifties.

###

CHAPTER 5

GETTING STARTED

THIS CHAPTER IS DEVOTED to the nuts and bolts of getting started as a trader or investor, beginning with where to go for information.

Sources of information

1. *Investor's Business Daily*

2. *Wall Street Journal*

3. *How to Make Money in Stocks* by William O'Neill

4. *Battle for Investment Survival* by Gerald Loeb

5. *One Up on Wall Street* by Peter Lynch

6. *Reminiscences of a Stock Operator* by Edwin Lefevre

7. *What I Learned Losing a Million Dollars* by Brendan Moynihan and Jim Paul

8. *Getting Started in Options* by Michael C. Thomsett

9. Any book (autobiography or biography) by or about Warren Buffett

###

There are myriad strategies you can employ. Pick one strategy that speaks to your persona and style, and then stick with it. The key is to develop a consistent investing routine and be disciplined with it.

Opening up a brokerage account

The top companies to consider are:

- ✓ Key point—low trading fees
- ✓ TD Ameritrade

- ✓ Scott Trade
- ✓ E-trade
- ✓ Fidelity
- ✓ Charles Schwab
- ✓ iShares
- ✓ Vanguard

The easiest, simplest way to grow or compound your wealth is to find a brokerage firm with low fees, set aside a portion of your income—ten percent or even more—and invest in index funds that have low fees and track the general market.

General mindset: what you're looking for

Decide on what type of stocks you want to invest or trade in:

- ➢ Growth versus value
- ➢ Long-term versus short-term
- ➢ Paying dividends
- ➢ Technicals versus fundamentals

How to Read a Chart

These are only the basics of reading a chart. When I read a chart, it helps me to decide if and when to get into a stock.

In general: Go with the trend. It is your friend.

Here are some of the key technical indicators that I use to spot bullish and bearish patterns:

Range: this is the price values the stock price fluctuates between over a certain time period or time range.

Support/resistance: these terms describe the price pattern of a particular stock. Support means the stock's price is less likely to fall than go up in value. Resistance means the price of a stock is likely at the top.

Volume: this is how many shares are being traded. The importance of this technical indicator is that you want to invest/trade a stock that is being actively bought and sold so, when it comes time to buy or sell, you can easily acquire or get rid of it.

I make a cutoff of one million shares. This is based on the law of supply and demand. A stock that has an actively traded volume of over one million shares will be more easily bought or sold at a fair price. The greater the spread between the bid and ask price, the greater the probability you will either buy too high or sell too low.

RSI (relative strength index): this value indicates whether a stock is overbought or oversold. The RSI oscillates between 0 and 100. A value over 70 is overbought; a value below 30 is oversold.

MACD: this is a technical indicator that indicates whether a stock is being bought or sold. It does not tell whether a stock is going to be bought or sold. It is just tells the direction the stock is either being bought or sold.

Convergence-divergence: a trading indicator that indicates the direction or momentum of a stock price (strong or weak). It does not tell whether the stock is going up or down; only the degree to which the stock is rising or dropping.

So, to sum it up, you can use your knowledge of value investing (how valuable the stock is relative to its price—P/E, price-to-sales, price-to-book ratio), dividend yield, and your knowledge of technical indicators to "predict" or forecast what directions the stock is going, in order to accurately assess if and/or when to get into or out of a stock.

A special note: these technical indicators reflect events after they have happened. Therefore, they are not *predictive*; only *reflective* of a stock's behavior.

###

CHAPTER 6

USING OPTIONS IN YOUR PORTFOLIO

THIS CHAPTER FOCUSES ON using options as an adjunct to maximizing your paper portfolio.

The advantages of using options include:

- ➤ Hedging
- ➤ Increasing gains exponentially
- ➤ Leverage; more for less
- ➤ Purchasing insurance on your stocks using options

- Trading based on market events (Fed interest rates, earnings, ex-dividend dates)
- Purchase a lot of shares at a specified price at a certain date
- Control versus ownership—when you purchase call options, you have control but don't possess ownership over the stock
- Getting paid to purchase a stock (selling cash secured puts)
- Getting paid to sell a stock (selling covered-calls in the money)
- Renting out your stock (covered-calls)

A great book that got me started along the options pathway was *Getting Started in Options* by Michael C. Thomsett. This book enlightened me to what was possible (infinite!).

Here are some definitions:

An *option* is the "right" to buy or sell a lot of stock shares at a certain price, at a particular set date in the future.

A *call option* is the right to sell a lot of shares at a specified price at a future date.

A *put option* is the right to buy a lot of shares at a specified price at a future date.

1 *contract* = 100 stock shares. Therefore, your leverage is 100:1 versus 1:1 with stocks.

When you own call and put contracts you control but don't own the shares.

Now, I know what you're thinking. How do I apply these definitions in real life?

I thought the same way. The best way that helped me to understand and apply these strategies was to think in terms of how does this apply, in real-life terms?

1. The *covered-call option* – *"renting out your stock."*

The covered-call strategy works well for predictable, stable stocks whose price falls within a channel. You must own stock in lots of 100 shares. Each month or week, you can sell one contract against your 100 shares and collect a premium. There are several scenarios that can play out, once you collect your premium:

A. You collect your premium and do nothing. If the price of the stock reaches the strike price, you are obligated to sell your lot of 100 shares, and your profit or loss is equal to the price you sold it at minus the purchase price, plus whatever premium you collected. If you want to continue owning the stock, even though you are obligated to sell it, you could buy back the covered-call contract at a loss and sell another covered-call option at a higher strike price in the near future.

B. If it is less than the strike price, you get to keep your premium, and you can rent out your stock again the next month or week. (At the time of the 2007 crash, the majority of covered-call contracts went uncalled; but in 2018, there is greater and greater market volatility.)

I used to sell contracts a month out in advance, but now, I look at weekly options contracts, since the price of stocks can fluctuate extremely widely in a span of days even hours.

C. The other thing you can do with your premium is buy either a put or a call contract, depending upon which way you think the stock will move. If the stock moves downward (i.e., loses money), you will offset that loss by making money with the put contract. And vice versa. If the stock moves upward and you purchased a call contract, you make money on both the stock and the call option. (That is what I call leverage.) I have had to use this strategy more and more often in today's market volatility.

The covered-call strategy does not work well for stocks poised for breakouts, because you get called out quite frequently. This simple concept is extremely powerful. Despite not learning about it during my first five years of investing experience, I was still able to become financially independent by the age of twenty-nine.

2. If I think the stock is going to move up or down ("*stocks on steroids*")...

I will look at the chart and identify the points of support and resistance for future dates.

I will purchase either a call or a put option (depending on whether I think the stock will move upward or downward) at a certain strike price, at a certain date. At the end of the period or beforehand, I will sell these call or put options, depending upon whether I made or lost money on my option.

This strategy works well for stocks that are on the rise or if there are any potential unplanned sudden price movements to the downside.

3. The *cash-secured put* — "getting paid to purchase a stock."

Let's say stock XYZ is $50 a share, and I have $4,000 to invest. I can, say, purchase stock XYZ at $50 a share; if I buy 100 shares, it will cost me $5,000. That is $1000 over my budget.

On the other hand, if I think $50 a share is too expensive or that XYZ is overvalued at this price, and if am willing to wait for a temporary dip, I can sell a cash-secured put at a strike price of $40. This way, I collect a premium, and if the price dips to$ 40, I can snap it up for a significant discount (both in the premium and via the $10 per share price dip). Note: this strategy is the same as the covered call, only in reverse.

4. *Naked calls and puts, straddles, collars, strangles.*

What do all of these fancy names mean? These are all advanced concepts that I have employed that led to my making a significant amount of money. However, there is high risk in using them, so it is not recommended for the beginning or average investor-trader (and is beyond the scope of this book).

If you're interested in more advanced techniques with stocks and options, send me a DM via social media to setup a free fifteen-minute private coaching session to determine which coaching program is best for you and how I can best serve your needs.

Now, I know what you are thinking, again. This is information overload. What I recommend you do is:

1. Take a break

2. Think about how and when to apply the different strategies. For example:

If the market is going up, you could:

    a. Buy call options, either for profit-gain, or to own the stock at the predetermined price

    b. Sell puts

If the market going down, you could:

    a. Buy puts as protection, insurance, or hedge

    b. Sell calls

If the market is in a sideways pattern, consider:

    a. Employing the covered-call strategy, or

    b. Buying on dips and selling on the gains (using stocks, calls, and puts)

If you own a stock at a certain price or want to take advantage of the ex-dividend date, you could:

    a. Buy a call option "in the money" and exercise the option in order to own a particular stock before the ex-dividend date.

    b. Sell a put "in the money" to own the stock before the ex-dividend date.

If you just employ the covered-call strategy, you can make yourself financially free. If you employ the above strategies, executed at the right time, you can make yourself extremely rich.

###

CHAPTER 7

MONEY MANAGEMENT

THIS IS A BRIEF OVERVIEW on money management. You should treat investing and trading much like a business.

I recommend you have starting capital of at least $250-500,000 plus two years' worth of living expenses in savings.

Keep track of your personal expenses and income, much like a regular business does. That being said, the amount you allocate to each position depends upon:

- ✓ the stock
- ✓ the trend
- ✓ the sentiment.

William O'Neill said that the key to success is to let your winners run and to cut your losers/short. The time you spend waiting for a particular stock to recover, you could be using to invest in winners.

My cutoff is a twenty-percent loss. Think about it: for every twenty-percent loss, you have to make a fifty-percent return, in order to make that loss back. For every fifty-percent loss, you have to make a hundred percent, to make that loss back. Therefore, you're better off cutting your losses and moving on.

But the average investor holds onto that position, only to lose out on other winners (remember the deprival super-reaction tendency cognitive bias above).

Risk and Management

This section is devoted to managing risk and investing wisely. Investing and trading are not gambling. Gambling is not adhering to a system, succumbing to fear, greed, and overconfidence, or taking wild risks.

The difference between an amateur and a professional is the following:

The amateur gambles. He/she is emotional, indulges in irrational behavior, acts on hunches, is ignorant, or is overconfident. They usually will get destroyed by their losses.

The professional investor and trader does his/her research-homework, adheres to a system, and manages his/her mental and emotional states, despite what is happening externally. He/she takes small, calculated risks, does not get too excited about wins or losses, and avoids irrational behavior.

While the professional investor sticks to a conservative, safe, and proven process, the amateur thinks about getting rich quick.

The tendency is to postpone taking losses (waiting for the loss to recover) and to take profits too early (versus letting your winners run).

Professionals develop a system, stay in for the long haul, and take calculated risks. They develop a trading system that includes daily, weekly, and monthly goals. They allocate only a certain percentage amount into certain categories.

Important ideas

- Know the difference between speculation versus investment
- Looking for quality management
- Looking for institutional investment
- Reinvesting the dividends
- Investment "advisors" are usually salesmen
- Develop a trading system
- Daily, weekly, monthly: allocate a certain amount percentage into certain categories

Setting rules for money management

- Let winners run.
- Cut losses quickly. The rule is, once they hit a 20% loss, the losers are cut and the funds are put into the winners.

- Only a portion of your portfolio on a trade. The rule is no more than a total of 2% of equity loss on any trade (cumulative), including fees.
- Take only small, calculated risks.

Tax saving strategies with a Roth IRA and solo 401(k)

I love Roth IRAs because it allows you to set aside a certain portion of your income every year, invest those funds, and withdraw them tax-free in your later years. There are certain limitations, however.

If your annual income is greater than the limits, you won't be eligible to contribute DIRECTLY into a Roth IRA. However, you can contribute to a traditional IRA and then convert it to a Roth IRA. This is known as a "back door" contribution. For 2019, the maximum Roth IRA contribution is $6,000. This is perfectly legal, and you must report this on your income tax return. There are tax advantages for opening an IRA versus a Roth IRA.

Consult your tax advisor, accountant, and estate-tax attorney.

For a solo 401k, you can contribute up to $19,000 for 2019, for a type 1 contribution. And you can make type 2 contributions up to a maximum of $56,000, depending upon whether your business is structured as a corporation or as a sole proprietor-partnership. The rules get tricky, so these are the general basics, and each situation applies differently.

Additionally, there are tax savings strategies with IRA, Simple IRAs, SEP IRAs, 403(b)s, Keogh, and 529 plans. Each individual has different financial pictures according to their own circumstances, so what works for me may be different for other people. Consult your tax attorney, tax accountant, and tax advisors.

###

CONCLUSION

STOCKS ARE A POWERFUL adjunct to your investing arsenal. This can be extremely powerful from a financial-independence standpoint.

Think about it: instead of you working for money, trading your time for assets, your money is working for you. Stocks are vehicles to massive wealth and riches.

However, you must have a plan, a system in place. You must know yourself, your wants, your strengths and weaknesses, and your goals, and you must have a plan of action to get there. You must exercise discipline.

In addition, this is an extremely scalable system. You must have a system for evaluating which stocks you want to incorporate into your plan—the vehicle—and then scale that. The more efficient and effective stocks you select, the better off you will be.

I have detailed the advantages and disadvantages of using stocks and options as a vehicle in your overall investment portfolio. I have described the amount of disruption our society is facing as a whole and likely will face, in the upcoming years. Those who are educated and prepared to embrace uncertainty and take advantage of opportunity will be the ones who benefit.

I have gone through the psychology of investment-trading, including maintaining a peak psychology and working in a peak state, plus the different types of biases that affect our decisions and behavior. I have looked at some of the technical aspects of when to get into and/or out of a particular trade. And I have given you an over my overview of options, which set me financially free at the age of twenty-nine.

Hopefully, you have found several of these myriad strategies useful and will put them to use. Remember: you must take action in order to be successful. The more action you take, the more successful you'll be.

Last but not least, I'd like to keep in touch with you. I offer private coaching and group coaching, in addition to the two books I've written. Reach out to me regarding about which products and services you're interested in, and either I or someone on my team will respond to you.

I am invested in your success. I wish, back in 2008, I'd had someone like myself to consult, someone with the amount of experience and wisdom I've accreted since then. Instead of toiling and struggling for eight whole years, I could have shaved four to five years off my learning curve.

Apart from totally immersing yourself with like-minded individuals, a coach is the surest, fastest, and easiest way to achieve your goals and dreams. You may say the price tag is too high, but the tradeoff is that you're using monetary resources to save time.

You can save the money and instead toil and struggle, but that will ultimately take more time in the long run.

Again, reach out to me at any time. I wish you continued success on our journey called life. In today's day and age, the greatest risk is not trying and failing, but not taking any risk at all, playing it safe, and, when you reach the end of your life, regretting your life, or wishing you could do it all over again instead of reaching out now and really going for your dreams.

###

ABOUT THE AUTHOR

DR. CHRISTOPHER LOO is a physician who became financially free at the age of twenty-nine and retired early at the age of thirty-eight, as a result of making strategic investments after the 2008 financial crisis. A graduate of the MD-PhD program offered jointly through the Baylor College of Medicine and Department of Bioengineering at Rice University, he is the author of *How I Quit My Lucrative Career and Achieved Financial Freedom*

Using Real Estate and three other Physician's Guides for financial freedom.

He is the host of the *Financial Freedom for Physicians* podcast, a regular contributor to KevinMD, and has spoken about the importance of financial literacy for Passive Income MD, the White Coat Investor, Board Vitals, SEAK Non-Clinical Careers, SoMe Docs, Doximity, Medpage Today, FinCon, and other high-profile financial brands geared toward high-income professionals.

His website is www.drchrisloomdphd.com.

###